THE LAZY MAN'S GUIDE TO RELAXATION

BY ISRAEL REGARDIE

oThe Tree and the Egyptian Gods
oThe Tree of Life
oThe Golden Dawn Tapes - Series I (Formerly THE REGARDIE TAPES)
oThe Golden Dawn Tapes - Series II
oGeomantic Divination
oTalismans and How to Make Them
oWhat You Should Know About The Golden Dawn
oThe Complete Golden Dawn System of Magic
oThe Teachers of Fulfillment
oThe One Year Manual
oThe Eye in the Triangle
oEnergy, Prayer and Relaxation
oCeremonial Magic
oThe Legend of Aleister Crowley
oLiber Nuts
oThe Qabalah of Israel Regardie
oThe Enochian Dictionary
oWilhelm Reich - His Theory and Therapy
oFoundations of Practical Magic
oThe Lazy Man's Guide to Relaxation
oStress Control and Relaxation
oThe Sceptre of Power
oRegardie Speaks

CROWLEY WORKS EDITED AND INTRODUCED BY ISRAEL REGARDIE

oRoll Away The Stone
oGems From The Equinox
oThe Best of Crowley
oRegardie narrating Crowley (Cassette Tape)
oThe Vision and the Voice

oMagick Without Tears
oThe Law is For All
oThe World's Tragedy
oAHA
oYoga

OTHER BOOKS FROM FALCON PRESS

oPrometheus Rising - Robert Anton Wilson
oThe New Inquisition - Robert Anton Wilson
oThe Tree - J. Marvin Spiegelman, Ph.D.
oThe Knight - J. Marvin Spiegelman, Ph.D.
oThe Quest - J. Marvin Spiegelman, Ph.D.
oThe Nymphomaniac - J. Marvin Spiegelman, Ph.D.
oJungian Psychology & Zen Buddhism - J. Marvin Spiegelman, Ph.D. and
  Mokusen Miyuki, Ph.D.
oZen Without Zen Masters - Camden Benares
oSurvival - Richard Van Praagh, M.D.
oThe Modern Jew In Search For His Soul - Abraham Jacobson, et al
oThis is it! It's How You Live it Now! The Endless Meditation
oUndoing Yourself with Energized Meditation - C.S. Hyatt
oThe Zendo - C.S. Hyatt

Inquiries into the availablilty of these books are welcomed by Falcon Press.

THE LAZY MAN'S GUIDE TO RELAXATION

By Dr. Israel Regardie

FOREWORD

By Bhagavan Jivananda

INTRODUCTION

By Robert A. Rosen, M.D.

1985

FALCON PRESS

PHOENIX, ARIZONA 85012, U.S.A.

International Standard Book Number:0-941404-28-5
Library of Congress Catalog Card Number:83-81835

Second Edition - Revised 1983
Second Printing - Falcon Press, 1985

Falcon Press, 3660 N. 3rd Street
Phoenix, Arizona 85012, U.S.A.
(602) 246-3546

Manufactured in the United States of America

CONTENTS

FOREWORD

"There once was a scholar of Chinese thought who came to visit a village which was suffering from a most unusual prolonged drought. All the people were very worried, since everything had been done to end it. Every kind of prayer, charm and magic had been used, but all to no avail. So the elders of the village told the old scholar that the only thing left was to send for the rainmaker.

The old scholar was very interested in this idea, since he had never seen a rainmaker before. The rainmaker arrived in a covered car. He was a small and wizened old man. He stepped out of the car and smelled the air in disgust. He then asked for a house on the outskirts of the village. He insisted that no one should disturb him and that his food should be placed outside his door.

No one heard or saw him for three days, when everyone was awakened by a heavy downpour of rain. It was even at times snowing, which was unusual for that time of year.

FOREWORD

The old scholar was deeply impressed and went to see him. The scholar asked, "So you can make rain?" The rainmaker scoffed at the idea and said "of course I can't." The scholar replied, "but there was the most persistent drought until you came, and within a few days it rains?" "Oh," replied the rainmaker, "that was something quite different. You see, I came from a region where everything was in order. It rains when it should and is dry when that is needed, and the people are also in order and Harmony with themselves. But that was not the case with the people here. They were all out of Harmony with themselves. I was at once ill when I arrived, so I had to be totally alone until I was once more in Harmony with myself and then of course quite naturally it rained!"

The essence of this little story is that when you are in Harmony with yourself the whole world begins to orchestrate with you. The *Lazy Man's Guide to Relaxation* is about finding this Harmony within yourself. You see, this is one of the great secrets of life, learning how to be in Harmony with yourself, and thus with the world. To do this -- to be in Harmony -- to be yourself -- you must first know how to relax. If you are truly relaxed everything begins to change. There is no need for deep penetrating thought -- only the Bliss of Relaxation.

In this little book written by a man with a vast knowledge encompassing various fields, the reader is treated to a nurturing and penetrating method of deep relaxation accomplished with simplicity and ease.

Now -- this is it! Let the portrait of the real you emerge, full of beauty, poise and confidence. The tensions of everyday life will drop away like so many leaves off a tree.

FOREWORD

After a few weeks of practice a new exhilaration will be yours. There will be joyousness in your heart and you will meet life with gaiety and vivacity. But, more importantly there will be peace of mind. You will be freed from the labour of worry.

So often the stress and strain of life makes us callous to friendship and love. We become short, sometimes even hostile. But it is very important never to forget that even though the frequent hardships of life cause pain, that asleep within -- is Harmony, the Being at one with everything -- the profound graceful source that can turn everything into a symphony of Joy.

Bhagavan Jivananda

INTRODUCTION

ROBERT A. ROSEN, M.D.

Mind, soul and spirit have always been vague and formless images. Matter, by contrast, is readily seen and touched. It was easier for early scientific analysis to deal with visible and tangible matter than the vague images just mentioned. Thus a differentiation came into being to separate mind and matter. This happened both on a religious level, a medical level, a psychological level, and a general practical level. In medicine, the body belonged to the physician; the mind to the psychologist, the spirit to the religious leader.

This may have been necessary in order to provide greater understanding of each separate aspect of the whole, but in the long run, and at our present stage of difficulties, it is a disturbing artificial creation.

Recently people have begun to realize that the differentiation between mind and matter is of little consequence.

11

INTRODUCTION

What happens when you make such a distinction is that you impoverish both sides since neither mind nor matter can function without the other. When you try to think of mind as immaterial or matter as mindless you get a philosophical mess on both sides. It is similar when we separate the medical point of view from the religious point of view. Both are losers. It is not only because they have lost their opposite half, but also because of the problem created when you separate a doctor from a priest. When you do that you create two specialties out of what was originally one field. This is very true historically. The original physicians and religious leaders were one and the same. We have found it necessary to separate them so as to be able to cleanse voodoo and superstition out of medicine. But we have also lost something. A true priest-physician is more than a priest plus a physician. He (or she) benefits from binocular vision that stems from medicine and from religion. The priest-physician sees not two areas, but one unified in three dimensions. Thus we can reunite the mind, body, and spirit to create a whole person, with better balance, and an ultimately better health.

We can reintegrate the effects of the mind on the body and the body on the mind without becoming confused.

Murphy and Leeds in 1975 showed that muscular tension, chronically inhibits the flood of painful memories which return if the individual relaxes. In other words when a person has a painful experience the energy of that experience is trapped within muscular tension. Before that relaxation has taken place the memories are not accessible to consciousness. But after relaxation a psychological re-organization occurs releasing the old blocked

INTRODUCTION

memories, thus allowing the person to release the muscle tensions which have caused backaches, neckaches, headaches, etc.

Many authorities have since confirmed the fact that anxiety cannot exist in the presence of deep muscular relaxation. Thus when one learns through a variety of techniques to relax the musculature the existence of anxiety is precluded and the empirical treatment of anxiety consists of simply reducing muscular tension.

Modern medicine has made some tremendous advances in the past century but especially in the last several years. Yet all of the new medications and procedures and new devices do not replace the sense of well-being that exist potentially within. Some of the art of the medical practice of years gone by must be revived in today's very stressful lifestyle. Dr. Regardie, many years ago wrote some important guidelines as to how one could let go of these superficial attitudes which produce distress, and return to the calm and peace and harmony associated with greater satisfaction and happiness that comes from being yourself.

He points out some important observations and techniques that one can use quite simply to help oneself in a way that no medicine of today or tomorrow can ever replace. One must remember that an ounce of prevention is worth at least a pound of cure. To all who are interested in the health and well-being of themselves, their families, and friends I recommend the reading of this book. Follow its advice and thus minimize future health problems and the need for the advanced technology of modern medicine required to treat diseases which relaxation could have prevented.

CHAPTER ONE

BE YOURSELF

Does this seem silly to you? You can't imagine being anyone else? Well, you're right, of course. You can't be someone else, but you can be considerably less than your true self. You can quite unconsciously be apeing another person altogether - one for whom you have had much love or admiration. Or, alternatively, you may be inhibiting yourself out of fear of life, or from a lack of knowledge of how to live. In such event, the real "you," whatever that actually may be, is prevented from obtaining creative expression.

This state of psychic inhibition in itself is productive of quite serious tensions in the spheres both of body and of mind. They are tensions of which, more likely than not, you have no direct awareness. It is through the impact of two opposite yet complementary forces that this involuntary tension gradually comes into being. For instance, there is on the one hand the dynamic tendency of self, or

LET THE REAL YOU OUT!

vital energy within, surging upwards and outwards all the time, seeking an opportunity to expend itself or find adequate expression in the external world. On the other hand, there is the effort upon the part of your own rather apprehensive ego to prevent the upward and outward surge of this dynamic instinctual creative force. After all, consciousness is a thing born from and trained by the restricting and peculiarly inhibiting nature of modern social organization. And, as well you know, life and present day society look askance at the unrestricted expression of the instincts regardless of the particular plane upon which they seek manifestation. There is the important factor of economic pressure. There is also the risk of social rejection and ostracism if one is too overt in verbal expression of one's feelings.

Moreover, if you happen to have artistic or creative abilities, no matter how well or ill-defined and developed, how much sympathy and assistance can you expect from those about you? Very little, I wager. In a few words, you - most of you reached by this book - are not being yourselves. A conflict is being waged within your own heart and mind. You are not in Harmony with nature. The first result of this, is that you are in a state of nervous and muscular tension from which you are unable to free yourself - believe it or not - even when you are resting or sleeping. Secondly, because of this you are wasting an enormous amount of energy and power which so easily could be employed in far more satisfying or creative directions. Very briefly, because of this inner conflict resulting in neuro-muscular tension, you find that you are unable to relax. Do you question this?

TO UNDERSTAND TRUE RELAXATION
PICK UP A SLEEPING CAT...

TOTAL RELAXATION IS POSSIBLE

Consider, then, the perfect power for rest in all animals. Lift up a sleeping cat. You will see how perfectly relaxed she is in every muscle. That is not only the way she sleeps, but the way she acts, rests, and relaxes. No matter how great or how intense the activity, when she stops she is able to drop every muscular tension. So it is with all animals, except in rare cases where man has tampered with them sufficiently to interfere with the true order of their lives.

THE LAZY MAN'S GUIDE TO RELAXATION

Watch a healthy baby sleeping. Lift one of its arms, its legs, or its head. You will find each perfectly relaxed and free. You can even hold it on your outspread hands, and the whole little weight, full of life, and gaining new power through the perfect rest, will give itself entirely to your hands, without one particle of tension. This, therefore, should serve as your ideal of rest. Were you able to "undo" yourself as completely as the cat and baby do, and lose yourself in a state of deliberate, consciously-induced relaxation, this tension would disappear by itself. You would then be free and healthy and well; you would be - yourself.

CHAPTER TWO

TENSIONS WASTE ENERGY

Let's try an experiment, you and I together. From this you will readily be able to realize whether or not what I have to say applies to you. It is not my intention to be dogmatic; you can prove everything I say or suggest. Lie flat on your back, either on the carpeted floor or on a bed. The former is preferable for the soft bed will yield, whereas it is you who should yield. Have a friend nearby to aid you in this experiment. The experiment can and should be reciprocated, and could be source of considerable pleasure for both of you. You can alternate who should be patient and who should be doctor.

Remain quite still for a few seconds with your eyes closed, trying your utmost to relax your entire body. Let your friend who is standing on your right side, take hold of your right leg under the ankle. Ask him to raise it six or seven inches in the air at an angle of about forty-five degrees, and drop it. Repeat this movement several times.

THE LAZY MAN'S GUIDE TO RELAXATION

This accomplished, let your friend raise your leg by the ankle, in the air. Before dropping it, let him place his other hand under the knee. If the right hand is holding the ankle, let the left hand be placed in the hollow space back of the knee, in what is technically known as the popliteal space. Remove the right hand. The probability is that your leg will remain flexed or extended in mid-air. It may take you some seconds to realize that you are holding it there. The leg is unsupported because your friend's hand has been removed, and in reality it is but the thigh which is being supported. The only conclusion to be arrived at is that your leg muscles have become involuntarily tense.

LEARN TO RELAX WITH A FRIEND!

Now it is obvious that energy is required to tense muscles. If your muscles are flexed or tense without your conscious knowledge or intention, just think of the vast quantity of energy with which you are prodigal; energy which, in short, you are wasting. Of course, if you are one of those unusually lucky people with an inexhaustible store of energy and are very vital and dynamic, it does not really matter very much. Actually, however, there are not many of these individuals. Most of us today, in the hectic rush of modern life, need to conserve our vitality. You and I need every ounce of the energy that we have in order to live and work and enjoy all the wonderful opportunities that life has placed before us in such a profligate manner.

THE LAZY MAN'S GUIDE TO RELAXATION

THE RAW FACTS

Since we in this country understand things so much better if we are given statistics, let me try and give you a few significant figures and facts which may assist your understanding. The body, like a locomotive, is primarily a machine. It is a complex mechanism capable of transforming the locked-up energy implicit in food, into the dynamic energy of work, motion, love and Harmony. A considerable amount of energy obviously is required to carry on even the internal work of the bodily mechanism of which we are not even aware. The so-called basal metabolism test now obsolete but replaced by more modern blood chemistry tests is one way of measuring how much energy we consume in vital bodily function. In reality, it measures your ability to inspire and utilize oxygen. Since all bodily functions depend upon oxygen consumption, it is thus possible to estimate whether you function too rapidly or too slowly; if your engine burns enough fuel or if it burns too much.

For example, in a resting man the heart utilizes about 10 per cent of the total energy intake in forcing the blood through the circulatory system. The diaphragm, and chest muscles, in order to maintain the movement of oxygen through the lungs, consume some 20 per cent of the total body energy. Here, remember, in only two of the several partial physiological systems of the body - the circulatory and respiratory systems - you consume practically one third of all the energy you have at your disposal. Ten per cent is utilized in the work of digestion and assimilation of the foods you eat, as well as in glandular action. About 35 per cent is used in the rapid, rhythmical muscular contractions by means of which bodily heat is maintained. Twenty per cent to 30 per cent is consumed in other vital work of excretion, reparation, reproduction and other vital functions. The set of facts involved is significant. Even when in a state of complete rest, as much as one-half of the total body energy expended may be traced to nothing but muscular tension under the stimulus of worry, fear, nervousness, or excitement of any kind, as well as other emotional activities.

EXHAUSTION

This form of energy expenditure may be increased to many times the normal amount. This explains why a person becomes tired, even to exhaustion, simply by waiting and doing nothing. For example, have you noticed how you react when you go to a dentist's office? The waiting-room seats three or four other people. This may mean a delay of about an hour before your turn arrives. Nothing could be simpler than to sit down, pick up one of the many magazines that you expect to find in such a room, and wait quietly. Instead, at the expiration of the hour, you feel utterly exhausted. Why? Because you have not sat quietly reading but were anticipating in your imagination the entire ordeal in the dentist's chair. Imaginatively, your are already in the chair enduring the tortures of the damned. It has been emotionally the equivalent of several visits to the dentist. With your mind so active, you have placed yourself in the chair, every muscle quivering with nervous energy, in a state of acute neuromuscular tension. Afterwards it becomes very difficult to "relax" and get rid of these tensions created by anxiety and anticipation. Here we have ample reason why a worried person or even a harried animal cannot be made to gain weight. It emphasizes the importance of complete rest as a favorable, even necessary factor, in increasing the body weight.

LEARNING TO RELAX

The ability to obtain complete rest is an art which, in spite of all their brilliance in the many fields of professional, scientific, and commercial endeavor, few people have mastered. Only an individual here and there has somehow retained from childhood the happy faculty of immediate relaxation. Rarer still is the individual who, having lost it in the turmoil of our modern, busy life, finds it again in the acquisition of a deliberate technique for so doing.

Unusual though the discovery of this technique is among the people we meet in every day life, it is abundantly clear that this rarity must be overcome. If you cannot relax and rest properly in order to give your nervous system the needed opportunity to recoup and recharge itself, you might just as logically throw your dinner, for example, out of the window to the dogs. You would get no nourishment this way. Similarly, by being unable to relax, your body is deprived of the opportunity to assimilate food and extract the necessary energy. Throwing your food away, as I suggest above, would be no more senseless than the ridiculous way in which most of us try to sleep or rest now. We wonder why we remain fatigued and exhausted after hours in bed. Yet this is the common experience of a good half of our population, certainly in the larger cities.

As Annie Payson Call wrote in her work *Power Through Repose* which is considered one of the great classics, but now unfortunately out of print: "Few who pretend to rest give up entirely to the bed, a dead weight, letting the bed hold them, instead of trying to hold themselves on the bed. Watch, and unless you are an exceptional case (unhappily there are few such), you will be surprised to see how you are holding yourself on the bed, with tense muscles; if not all over, so nearly all over that a little more tension would hardly increase the fatigue with which you are working.

"The spine seems to be the central point of tension; it does not give to the bed and rest there easily from end to end; it touches at each end and just so far along from each end as the man or woman who is holding it will permit. The knees are drawn up, the muscles of the legs tense, the hands and arms contracted, and the fingers clenched, either holding the pillows or themselves.

"The head, instead of letting the pillow have its full weight, holds itself onto the pillow, The tongue cleaves to the roof of the mouth, the throat muscles are contracted, and the muscles of the face drawn up in one way or another."

I do not want to burden you or terrify you with fearful descriptions of tension or with sets of useless figures. But it is urgent to emphasize this matter of bodily activity or metabolism using up vital energy. It is upon this one consideration, that my entire thesis depends: the absolute necessity for relaxation.

THE DEMANDS OF MODERN LIFE

If so much of our own substance and energy is being constantly expended because the demands of modern life are so exacting, exhausting, and wearing, we must have a simple technique which predisposes toward an easy relaxation of our faculties. It must be able to relax both our bodily functions and ourselves generally, in order that a speedier recuperation of vital function be established.

The technique I propose to delineate here does precisely this. It is very simple. All unnecessary and complicated details have been eliminated so as to render it usable by the average man and woman, who, like myself, have obligations to render to life and family. The little experiment suggested almost at the outset should have shown you how urgent is your need for relaxation. Try two or three more little experiments in this direction, and see how much your body not only requires it but actually desires it. I say "desire" advisedly. After a few seconds of this posture, lying flat on your back, you will experience such a comfort, such an exquisite sense of relief - yes relief - that you will actually heave a series of very deep sighs. It is as though an enormous weight were taken off your chest and your mind were lifted of a terrible burden. You will feel light, almost gay and happy.

THE LAZY MAN'S GUIDE TO RELAXATION

Your body needs relaxation. If these vital metabolic processes delineated in the foregoing paragraphs are to continue adequately and satisfactorily, none of this precious energy must be wasted in unnecessarily tensing muscles that are not being employed. Why are those abdominal muscles taut just now? Those shoulder and neck muscles, why should they be rigid as, while reading, you lean your head against the wing of your reclining chair? There is no need to do this at all. You must now begin to learn something of the gentle and invaluable art of relaxation.

GETTING ACQUAINTED WITH THE BODY

A few minutes, once or twice a day, spent in relaxation will work wonders. You will eventually come to realize that you should have done this long ago. Carry out your experimental work with a friend or someone living with you; someone who too would like to learn how to relax, for then you can work reciprocally and be a help to each other.

THE LAZY MAN'S GUIDE TO RELAXATION

Lie down on something hard, a wooden bench or on a rug covered floor. There you will be confronted by the psychological crisis which is so desirable. You will find the floor so thoroughly uncomfortable that you will soon become aware of the tautness and tensions of your own body; and consequently, make the effort toward eliminating them. The floor will not give no matter how good the rug so it will have to be you. In my own former practice I found a good hard bench (like a massage table or a diagnostic bench) with only a minimum of padding or cushioning, is most effectual in order to teach the subject.

Here you are then, lying down on a hard surface. Take a few very deep sighs, the sort of sigh you would heave if your heart were breaking. At once you discover a certain degree of loosening-up occurring. If the diaphram and abdominal muscles relax, the greater part of the muscles and tissue supplied by the involuntary nervous system, too, will loosen up with it. Lie quietly like that for a few seconds, observing yourself all the time. Become familiar with the body; learn to notice what the body feeling is like. In all probability, you have never had any awareness of what your own physical body feels like. Of course, we all know we have two arms, two legs, a heart, liver, and lungs, and so forth. There have been occasions, no doubt, when indigestion has made you aware of stomach discomfort. This sort of awareness is pathological and unhealthy. Once the cause is eliminated, once you overcome the symptoms of indigestion or biliousness, with it vanishes the awareness. All bodily activities sink back once more into complete unconsciousness where they rightly belong. During the process of relaxation you learn to recognize the distinctive physical sensations that accompany your body. Your body is like a friend or marriage partner with whom you spend your life. You live with it, eat with it, relax with it, sleep with it all your life. Such being the case, you may as well learn its whims and caprices, its peculiar tendencies and characteristics, learn to accept and humor them; learn to co-operate and work with them. The body will do the same for you. You will be surprised to find what a good friend, what a faithful, loyal servant, your body can be.

During these experiments watch yourself and watch your body. Be keenly observant when you relax. You will enjoy it after a while. It is actually an introduction into a new world.. This new world, however, is no new continent, no strange intriguing field like electronics or mechanics, or even the films or the theatre. This new world is only you. You will discover that you never really knew yourself. You have been all your life a stranger to yourself. No outsider is needed to introduce you to this intriguing stranger. Make the effort and the introduction takes place automatically. When you come to know yourself well and familiarly, you will be grateful to have learned this art of relaxation. These, then, are the first preliminary steps. Lie down on some hard surface. This makes you aware of how unrelaxed your are. Heave a few deep sighs from deep down in the abdomen. These steps will go far toward ensuring the induction of some degree of real loosening up. Moreover, you can do this by yourself.

CHAPTER THREE

AN EXAMPLE OF RELAXATION

In order to make as clear as possible the steps involved in this techinque, I shall describe a typical session with a patient whom we'll call Mr. A. Mr. A. had undergone a thorough physical examination in an effort to find out why he was always tired, why he had no energy, why his nerves were on edge. The examination had shown him to be in perfect physical condition, with no organic disorder. When it was suggested to him that he was always tired because he never relaxed, he had been skeptical. But he continued to be tired and had finally decided that it couldn't do any harm to look into this matter of relaxation. So now he was lying on my treatment table, waiting for me to show him what I was talking about.

"Sigh," I suggested. "What?" His tone was bewildered. "Sigh. Deep sighs, from way down in your abdomen." He complied somewhat self-consciously. "Now close your eyes," I said. "Stop watching me; forget about the pictures on the wall. Close your eyes and just think about how you feel." He closed his eyes, and drew another sigh for good measure.

"I'm going to pick up your right leg by the ankle," I said, "and then let go of it. Don't try to stop it from falling. Just loosen up the muscles and let it drop." Several times I picked up the right leg, and let it fall heavily to the table. I did the same with the left leg. After I had done it repeatedly, Mr. A. asked, in some surprise, "Is this all there is to relaxing?"

"Oh, no, this is just the beginning." I picked up his right leg again, but instead of dropping it, I put one hand under his knee, a couple of inches up on the thigh, before I removed my other hand from his ankle. Instead of dropping at the knee, as it should have the leg remained rigid, extended at a 45 degree angle. After a moment Mr. A. opened his eyes. "What's the matter?" he asked. "What are you stopping for?" I indicated the rigidly extended leg. "Why are you holding it up?" I asked.

"I thought you were holding it up." He started to bend his knee, but I stopped him.

"No, I don't want you to use muscular energy to force it down. What I want you to do is withdraw nervous energy from those muscles by thinking. It's involuntary tension that's keeping that leg up in the air. As soon as you become conscious of it, it ceases to be involuntary, and is then under your control. It is involuntary tension, all over your body, that's been keeping you tired. Now let's try the other leg." I picked up his left leg, slipped my hand under his knees, and then let go of the ankle. The left leg began to bend at the knee.

"You see," I said encouragingly, "how quickly you're learning to relax? What you just learned from your right leg, you've begun to apply to the left one. As a matter of fact, the whole secret of successful relaxation is nothing but self-awareness. Once you become aware of these tensions, it's within your power to eliminate them, to cease to waste energy by keeping your muscles uselessly tense." Mr. A. laughed. "I can certainly think of better ways of using up energy. What about the rest of me? Can you take the kinks out of my back and shoulders the way you have out of my legs?"

"Certainly. The 'kinks' come from nothing more than a perfectly useless resistance to the pull of gravity. Here let me show you how it works in your hip muscles." Grasping his ankles with one hand, I raised his legs, slid the other hand under his knees, and let go of the ankles. The lower leg dropped, his feet were flat on the bench - much the position one assumes when propping a book against the knees while reading in bed. I put one hand on his feet, to hold them still, and with the other gave his knees a slight shove to the right. They moved an inch or so, then stopped when I let up the pressure. "See what I mean about resisting the pull of gravity?" Mr. A. considered for a moment. "You mean my knees ought to tumble right over?"

"Certainly. There's nothing to stop them except the tension in your hip muscles. Now that you know the tension's there, you can relax it. Let's try it again." Once more I gave his knees a slight push to the right. There was a momentary resistance, then they tumbled over quite loosely. "You see how simple it is?" He grinned.

"Yeah, nothing to it. After you know." I pulled his knees up again, and pushed to the left. This time they responded immediately. I moved them up the center again, and separated the knees. They fell outward to their respective sides. After I'd repeated this several times, the tenseness in the heavy, powerful muscles of the thighs and hips was completely gone. Straightening out his legs, I took hold of his right hand and shook it gently, up and down and sideways. Then I rested the elbow on the bench, and held the forearm straight up by the finger tips. I removed my hand. The forearm remained extended in mid-air. Politely I inquired, "What are you pointing at?" Mr. A. glanced at his arm and grinned again. "Same old thing, eh? No wonder I was tired." As he spoke, his forearm dropped to the bench with a thud.

"That's more like it." I reached across him and repeated the same performance on his left arm. Mr. A. watched, and the tension went out of the left arm a great deal faster than it had with the right. "You see," I said, "It's just a matter of knowing when your muscles are tense. When you know it, you can remove the energy that's tensing them, or not, just as you wish. Energy used in keeping muscles tense when there's some good reason for their tenseness isn't wasted energy. But when you use up nervous energy keeping muscles tensed without knowing they are tense - that's a pretty silly way of using up energy you need for other things, isn't it?" I lifted his right arm by the finger tips again, and because of the conscious relaxation, it fell immediately when I let go of it.

"It feels like three sacks of flour, now." Mr. A. commented. "My upper arm and forearm and hand all feel heavy and loose, when you let go."

"That's the way they should feel," I answered. "Now, I want you to shrug your shoulders - one shoulder at a time." He tried to follow, but both shoulders moved together. "One at a time," I repeated. "Half a dozen times with each shoulder." After a short struggle he succeeded in breaking the habitual co-ordination that made his shoulders move simultaneously. After he had loosened them up somewhat by this method, I helped him by gripping each shoulder and moving them up and down, one at a time, with considerable vigor. Then I pulled each shoulder, alternately, toward me, away from the bench, and released it quickly. His body dropped heavily back to the bench, his head waggling. After I had repeated the movement several times with each shoulder, the waggling of the head became more pronounced, indicating that the neck muscles were relaxing more and more. Mr. A. heaved a sigh of contentment.

"It's amazing," he said, "how quiet and poised I feel inside. That nagging, nervous feeling is practically gone." I nodded. "To my mind, that's the test of true relaxation. But this is only the beginning. We're going to attack another set of tensions now." With my finger tips, I located the top of the hips - the bone called the ilium. Then I slipped my fingers off its uppermost point, the crest near the anterior superior spine, downward to the right side to the fleshy and muscular part of the abdomen, and pressed on it, not too heavily. I repeated the same process on the left side. Press and release, press and release, several times. Then, with the flat of my hand, I pressed gently into the abdomen just above the region of the navel. Immediately, the muscles under my hand contracted. "Does that hurt?" I asked. Mr. A. shook his head. "No. Should it?" I smiled at the question. "No, it shouldn't hurt. But I couldn't tell, when those muscles tensed up, whether it was because I was hurting you, or whether it was just defense mechanism - an automatic attempt on your part to protect the soft parts of the body by tensing the muscles that shelter them. It's equivalent to the mental attitude that many people have toward life - an attempt to escape pain by enclosing themselves in an iron wall of defense. It's an admission of fear - or at least a lack of courage.

TENSION IS PAIN

Remember always that pressure will only hurt if you resist it. The more tense you are, the more pain is felt from the pressure. That's a general principle that can be to a good many aspects of living." Mr. A. nodded appreciatively. "I get your point there. I'll try to keep it in mind." He paused a moment, then observed, "Golly, I feel good." He breathed a deep, contented sigh. I laughed. "You sound more as though your heart were broken."

"Yeah, I noticed that - I can't seem to keep from sighing. It's a funny thing, though - every time I sigh, I feel that much better. Sort of quiet, inside." I nodded. "I've been wondering if you'd noticed that. It's an excellent symptom, for each sigh, besides being an expression of relaxation, contributes toward a deeper relaxation. The more you sigh, the quieter you'll feel."

"It's almost as good as being asleep," Mr. A. murmured drowsily.

"Better, in fact, because when I'm asleep I can't appreciate how good it feels."

I placed my hands on his ribs, just under the breasts, then exerted a slight pressure as he exhaled. Maintaining the pressure, I said, "You've probably never realized how completely flexible and mobile your breathing apparatus is - the lungs, themselves, the chest, the rib cage. If one part of the mechanism is prevented from moving, another part will move instead. Emotional tension and other inward difficulties make the whole thoracic cage stiff and inflexible. Have you noticed what's happened to your breathing since I started this pressure on your ribs?"

"Yes - I seem to be breathing exclusively with my abdomen - and a few moments ago, when you were leaning on my stomach, I was breathing just under my collar bones."

"That's exactly what I was telling you - if you prevent one part of your breathing apparatus from moving, another part will move instead. When you breathe abdominally, the chest muscles, temporarily unused, must relax. When I place my hands in the middle of your chest and press gently downwards, this calls your attention to the tensions of the chest muscles - and as you have found out, awareness of tension is all that's necessary to eliminate it. Now, we've just about finished with the loosening up - we'll give your head the last touch."

"I thought you fixed my neck up when you were doing my shoulders," said Mr. A. "Anyway, it feels good now."

"Well, we'll check on it, anyway." I lifted his head, slipped my other hand under it to protect it, and used the same technique I'd used on his legs - and dropped it. Rolling it gently from side to side, I raised and dropped it several times. The stiff, awkward movement that indicated resistance and tension disappeared rapidly. I stepped back from the bench.

"How do you feel now?" Mr. A. stretched luxuriously, and didn't even bother to open his eyes. "As though my body were a comfortable place to live in, for a change, instead of a heavy, aching burden I had to drag around with me."

CHAPTER FOUR

CREATIVE RESULTS OF RELAXATION

At this juncture the person quite often goes fast to sleep. It is best to let him do so. It lasts for a few minutes and is most refreshing. It is as though the relief induced by the elimination of gross tension is too much to be borne, and sleep logically develops. Again, we may say that all through our lives there is such a complete identification of mind and body that we are unable to conceive of ourselves as apart from the body and its activities. When obvious bodily activities cease, because of false associations we imagine ourselves too as ceasing to exist, and lapse forthwith into the unconsciousness of slumber. Whilst relaxing, no body movements are taking place. It is as though the entire personality succumbs to its habitually conditioned reaction of falling into sleep when there is no activity to keep it focused on the outside world.

But this is a reaction which is soon overcome. Repeated experience of the relaxed state brings with it acclimatization. One becomes accustomed to living in and with a relaxed frame which is not exhausting its vital energies in maintaining unnecessary and useless tensions. That vital energy, therefore, being retained within, goes towards heightening and clarifying the mind. Energy must do something. Energy is defined as that which can perform work. If energy is not being wasted in keeping your neck or your abdomen or thigh rigid and taut, it is still retained within your own system. What happens to the energy therefore? In physics, as I have remarked, energy is considered very concretely as that which will do work. Now, if you are relaxed and there is no needless expenditure of metabolic energy, that energy must do something. Hence, the work it does is entirely psychological in nature and scope. All your latent abilities and mental powers and faculties become sharpened. A distinct exaltation must accompany the process. There should be a fresh acquisition of intellectual power and capacity.

THE LAZY MAN'S GUIDE TO RELAXATION

We might liken the phenomenon to a process of incubation. The energy remaining within starts to "hatch" you. Your personality becomes bolder and more clearly defined. So much so, that other people may even notice it. You may even be asked what has happened to you. Especially may people notice the poise and the repose which you are showing. They will envy and respect you for it. This will be the most obvious result from your effort, and this you will find to be extremely worth while; worth all the effort you may have expended.

WHEN YOU ARE BY YOURSELF

To the method described above, one requiring at first the assistance of another person, let me add another method, simpler in a sense, designated for self-operation. It was worked out many years ago by a brilliant relaxation exponent, and it is sufficiently excellent to warrant inclusion here at some length.

"After the deep breathing, drag your leg up slowly, very slowly, trying to make no effort except in the hip joint, allowing the knee to bend, and dragging the heel heavily along the floor, until it is up so far that the sole of the foot touches the floor without effort on your part. Stop occasionally in the motion and let the weight come into the heel, then drag the foot with less effort than before - so the strain of movement will be steadily decreased. Let the leg slip slowly down, and when it is nearly flat on the floor again, let go, so that it gives entirely and drags from its own weight. It is perfectly free, there is a pleasant little spring from the impetus of dropping, which is more or less according to the state of health of the body. The same motion must be repeated with the other leg. Every movement should be slower each day.

"It is well to repeat the movements of the legs three times, trying each time to move more slowly, with the leg heavier than the time before. After this, lift the arm slowly from the shoulder, letting the hand hang over until it is perpendicular to the floor. Be careful to think of the arm as heavy with the motive power in the shoulder. It helps to relax if you imagine your arm held to the shoulder by a single hair, and that if you move it with a force beyond the minimum needed to raise it, it will drop off entirely.

"After the arm is raised to a perpendicular position, let the force of gravity have it. First the upper arm to the elbow, and then the forearm and hand, so that it falls by pieces. Follow the same motion, with the other arm and repeat this three times, trying to improve with each repetition."

The same result for the head and body can be procured by rolling from side to side a few times.

In my own former professional practice, the first experiment in relaxation goes no further than what has just been described; the testing or probing of tension. This I call the first session's work. When the patient comes a second time, the same procedure is gone through, but very quickly. If the tensions are severe, as is often the case, the whole period is devoted to a repetition of proving, and no new work is undertaken. Three or four sessions are often devoted to the same process. When I find that tensions are very largely eliminated, the patient is ready to go forward, and we begin to work out a plan for the next phase of deepening or heightening the awareness of a relaxed body.

As we stated in the foregoing, the second session is begun by repeating the act of testing the condition of the muscular tensions, making certain that the grosser tensions have been completely eliminated. For example, if an arm is raised, it should drop easily and dully when my restraining hand is removed. If the abdomen is gently prodded, I do not expect to find a rapid reflex response in that area, etc. We test similarly, hands, feet, chest and abdomen, neck and shoulders. All are relaxed. The patient is lying quiet and still; arms are flung outwards on the bench or couch in spread-eagle fashion. Legs are spread several inches apart. The patient looks like a young child whom you surprise on a chance visit to the nursery. There, on his bed is the child with his little limbs flung, as it were, in every direction, completely at ease and relaxed. This posture is well enough for children and youngsters. They have unlimited supplies of energy, and can afford to waste it in playing vigorously, exercising, and sleeping in this spread-eagle manner. But do you realize that if you, an adult, were to sleep that way, you would be throwing off long streamers of energy?

THE VERIFICATION OF RESULTS

I do not want you to take my word alone for the statements I happen to make. The description of each step with its psychological reactions is absolutely open to verification by every one of you. The subject of relaxation is strictly scientific. So far as concerns this question of energy, observe rather closely the habits of old people. When next you visit your grandparents or other elderly people, notice how they sit when they are resting. You notice first, that their feet are crossed at the ankle. If you look closer, you see their hands are clasped with fingers interlocked. The hands rest on the solar plexus just under the stomach, or in the lap. They seem to be resting easily and well this way and are altogether comfortable. What is the significance of these two postures? The child with extremities spread-eagled and flung in every direction, and the aged person with feet crossed at the ankles (legs crossed at the knee would produce a deleterious effect on the circulation of the blood), and the fingers interlaced over the stomach? The significance should be clear. The growing child is endowed by nature with a super-abundance of energy. This he does not bother to conserve and is as lavish in its expenditure as nature has been prodigal in pouring her other gifts upon him. The older person, on the other hand, does not have this surplus of vitality. He now feels there is a necessity for conserving it and making the best use of what little vitality he has left. All this is indicated by the pose, the method of resting.

What is important is the question whether or not this observation has any practical value so far as we are concerned. We are trying to learn how to relax and to eliminate tensions from the body, mind, and system, so as to make better use of the dynamic currents of energy coursing through us in order to live more happily and to know ourselves better. We want to be ourselves in order to better and more fully live life. Energy - and abundance of energy - is necessary if we are to live and function to our best advantage.

Not only is this indicated, but we also are shown the way of achievement. So we take advantage of this observation practically and pragmatically. The next step proceeds in this manner: The patient is relaxed and spread-eagled on the massage bench, or, if you are following me step by step, you are on the hard, rug-covered floor. A large pillow is rolled and slipped under the knees, raising them somewhat. The feet are crossed at the ankles in such a way that both heels rest on the bench. I take both hands (patient does not assist me) and interlace his fingers myself. I place them between the navel and the end of the sternum or breast-bone. No pillow is under the head, unless the patient is stout or has a tendency to cardiac decompensation. In that case, a small pillow or cushion is placed under the neck and back part of the head. This is the only exception. Without a word, I permit the individual to remain in this position for about a minute.

Again, without the utterance of a single word I "undo" him. Legs and arms are again spread-eagled. There he lies on the bench with limbs flung in every direction. He remains in this position for a minute. He is again "done up," which is my expression for crossing the ankles and interlacing the fingers on the stomach. Again and again I repeat this process without any remarks to the patient. Eventually I ask him in which of these positions he felt most comfortable. "Do you feel most still and comfortable spread-eagled? Or is the relaxation more profound with the arms and legs crossed?" Invariably, the answer is that with the legs crossed and fingers interlaced there is a greater degree of comfort and inner warmth, as well as a strong sense of satisfaction, even pleasure. This process I have repeated again and again. There is no doubt in my mind that here we are confronted by an absolutely scientific fact, whatever the explanation of the fact is. By so crossing the legs and interlacing the fingers which, by the way, is an old meditation posture - we produce a kind of closed electrical circuit wherein the circulating energy turns in upon itself and revolves as it were in its own closed nervous system. When this closed magnetic sphere is produced, then we are confronted by another equally interesting phenomenon.

It is known that power produces power - just as wealth will go on producing and increasing wealth. In this case, energy turned in upon itself gradually generates an increasing abundance of energy. It seems to the patient, while relaxing in this way, that his store of energy actually creates a distinct surplus. His posture almost converts him to a "step-up" transformer. So pronounced does this become that it may prove impossible to remain in the relaxed state, and it becomes necessary to get up and do something.

THE IMPORTANCE OF SOUND SLEEP

In one sense, this cannot be due to the mere cessation of active work and movement. We know there are occasions for many of us when sleep, which is a cessation of active work, does not bring us the refreshment and recharging of energy that we would expect of it. There are many factors to account for this. Over-fatigue, which is one explanation, is only part of the story. Inner psychic conflicts and struggles within the mind itself which use up our reserves of energy and exhaust us - there are other phases of the story. Both over-fatigue and psychic conflicts create neuromuscular tension. For muscles to remain tense, energy must be used. Hence, in a state of chronic muscular contractions, our normal reserves of energy are very much eaten into and consumed. Thus, chronic fatigue is produced - a very dangerous state. Then each organ is involved in a fatigue syndrome. The wits become dull, the memory impaired, and the ability to learn is very markedly decreased.

" EVEN WHILE ASLEEP, THE BODY IS HARD AT WORK! "

Actually, during complete rest, even during sound sleep, the body cells in various organs and tissues are hard at work. The heart muscles continue to beat regularly and to pump blood through the arteries; there is the rhythmical inhalation and exhalation of the oxygen in the lungs; the body heat is maintained and distributed by oxidation in the cells themselves; liver action and kidney excretion, as well as many other functions are continued. All the general metabolic functions are performed as before, all demanding the expenditure of a terrific amount of energy. Sleep and rest, therefore, imply work. It probably costs us almost more measurable energy to repair our bodies - to eliminate toxins, to rebuild and develop broken down tissues - than it costs to use them. The chief requirement of sound sleep is that it should permit adequate reparation. That is, it should permit the body to recoup itself, to elevate the reserves of cellular vitality, and thus generate more energy for general somatic utilization.

When tension and contraction are habitual states of life; when muscles and nerves are involuntarily taut and rigid, there is an impediment of the ability of the body to repair itself. Contraction of muscles wastes nervous and muscular energy. It hinders the free circulation of blood by impeding normal dilation of arteries, strains and overworks the heart, and moreover restricts breathing and other functions related to it. If you think that upon going to sleep a spontaneous relaxation occurs, I am afraid you will find yourself greatly disappointed when you come to observe or perform experiments upon the majority of sleeping people. But while relaxed in the manner I have indicated, with arms and legs placed in a comfortable position permitting the interaction of bodily energy, tension and contraction tend to disappear. This permits a freer circulation of blood, a slowing down of the overworked heart, and an easier inspiration of the breath. Cell reproduction and rebuilding of tissue can therefore continue without too great an expenditure of energy. The body's own alchemical laboratory will go on generating more power and energy itself. You may possibly disagree with my formulation of the observed facts or with any of my physiological explanations. That is unimportant. You must experiment yourself with your own body to obtain relaxation and observe these incidents, sensations, and psychological phenomena. Explain them afterwards if you wish. First relax.

CHAPTER FIVE

VISUALIZATION IN RELAXATION

So far, so good! You may begin now to compliment yourself on the degree of relaxation obtained, to revel in the sense of comfort and ease and poise resulting therefrom. Unfortunately, you are only beginning. This technique can be carried considerably further. We now extend it in a slightly different direction.

Heretofore, we have relied exclusively upon physical methods of inducing the giving-up of tensions. Now we approach it from an entirely different angle - the ability of your own mind to produce an effect upon the physiology of your body. A little later I shall enter this matter more thoroughly. For the moment, these are the facts: you are encouraged to try them out for yourself. Having experimented, you will then appreciate the force of my remarks. Once again I shall resort to an interview between myself and a supposed patient. I do so to assist enormous indentation in the bench you're lying on, and your own understanding of the process. It will be a slight matter to translate this into a similiar experience between you and a friend or a relative - anyone who is co-operating with you. Mr. A. lay on the massage table, his feet crossed, his fingers interlaced. His breathing was deep and regular; every now and then he sighed. Contrary to the romantic, fictional interpretation, sighs indicate contentment and relaxation quite as frequently as they reveal a troubled soul. In Mr. A.'s case the relaxation already induced by the physical methods employed had resulted in the dropping of his burden of nervous and muscular tension - a ridiculous burden which culminates in nervous exhaustion. The relief and pleasure resulting were expressed by those sighs. When he spoke, which he did reluctantly, it was in a quiet tone, very different from the high-pitched, nervous speech he had used when he came into the office. I pulled up a chair beside the bench he lay on. "Are you right-handed?" I asked. "Yes. Why?"

"If you weren't, I'd sit on your left, instead of here." I placed my left hand on the crown of his head, my right hand under his interlaced fingers on his solar plexus. "Don't move," I said. "Don't make any effort. Just observe yourself for a minute or two, and let me know whether my linking myself to you this way improves your relaxation and deepens your sense of comfort." Mr. A. was quiet for a few minutes. Then he said, somewhat inaudibly, "Yes, definitely. I'm even more relaxed - and I didn't think that was possible. I don't even want to talk. I could go right to sleep."

"Don't do that just yet," I said. "I want you to use your imagination. Pretend that you're very heavy - that you weigh three or four tons. Imagine that you're making an that in just a moment you'll be pulled right through the floor by gravity." Mr. A. was silent for quite a long time. Then he said, "I didn't think I could feel any more relaxed - but I do."

"Relaxation is an art; like other arts, the more you practice, the more proficient you become. After your physical relaxation has reached its peak, you'll have the task of mental relaxation to deal with. But the more relaxed you are physically, the easier it is to relax mentally - the two work hand in hand."

"You know," said Mr. A. thoughtfully, "one funny thing I've noticed is a sort of detachment I never experienced before - as though my body were separate from me - it's a sort of awareness of my body as a thing itself, instead of an integral part of me." I nodded. "That's good - that proves that the relaxation is doing what it's supposed to do. And you'll find your awareness of the body mounting and mounting. Eventually, it will reach a sort of peak, a crescendo of pure feeling, and then it will fall away from you altogether. The sense of body will disappear, and you will become aware of yourself -aware of you, as you really are, and not of the body and its organs and functions which you have always thought of as you. Actually, it's a sort of release from emotional and muscular bondage." "I'm not sure I know what you mean," said Mr. A. doubtfully.

"You will," I assured him. "Now, I want you to call on your imagination again. You know what a skein of wool looks like, with all the threads hanging loose from the fingers when you dangle the skein in the air?" Mr. A. nodded. "Yes, I can picture that."

"Fine. Now I want you to imagine your muscles as so many skeins of wool, all dangling loosely from a fixed point. For example, think of the muscles in your foot, extending from the ankle to the toes. Think of them as several strands of fibres, dangling from the ankle. Close your eyes and concentrate on the picture, and tell me what happens." Mr. A. was silent for several seconds. Then he said, in a tone of considerable surprise. "That's funny. After I had thought about my foot for a few moments, I swear I could feel a sort of loosening up, a warm, tingling feeling, right down to my toes."

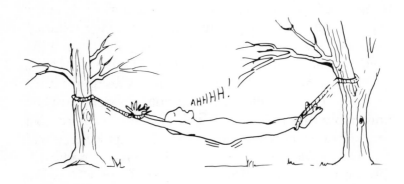

"That's splendid - that's what I wanted you to do. You've thought relaxation into the area you were concentrating on. Now carry on with the same idea in other regions. For example, the muscles hanging from the knee cap down to the ankle; from the hip bone to the knee; the muscles on the abdomen; around the chest, following the direction of the ribs from the breast bone round to the spine; the muscles along the back on each side of the vertebrae. Imagine these fibers dangling easily and freely from the neck. Then, finally, the muscles of the neck and shoulders; arms, forearms and hands. Take your time doing this, then stop and notice the sense of freedom and release that comes from it."

I waited patiently while Mr. A. struggled with this unaccustomed demand on his imagination. Finally he sighed and said, "I see what you mean. It produces the same feelings as I had when you began calling my attention to the tensions in my legs and arms."

ACTIVE IMAGINATION

This completes the second stage. The third stage of the process is similar insofar as we employ actively the imagination. There is a well-known physiological law that an increased flow of blood to any part of the body can be produced by concentrating on that part of the body. Whether it is merely becoming conscious of the blood already in the vessels there, or that nervous impulses are conveyed to the muscular wall of the veins and arteries in the area contemplated, thus relaxing those walls and permitting an increased flow of blood through an enlarged lumen - all this is unimportant. That this can be done is an accredited fact. For example, you say to a small child that she is pretty. If unaccustomed to such compliments she will likely blush. Blushing is the result of an increased supply of blood flowing to the vessels of the face and neck. You have made her conscious of her little face and this consciousness produces the effect noted. Although for her this is an involuntary neurological phenomenon, nevertheless, the fact is of tremendous significance. This is a law we ourselves can utilize in a wholly constructive way with regard to our task of relaxation.

If we know that there are tensions in a certain limb or organ, we can by thinking about it, stimulate vasodilator nerve fibres which relax blood vessels and cause the blood to flow there. A surplus amount of blood or a congestion will cause a degree of heat which, in turn, will produce the relaxation of muscular fibre and tissue that we desire. Just as the muscles responded to your visualization of them as threads of wool, so also will the blood stream respond to your imagination and flow just where you want it to.

Let us play with the idea, using Mr. A. again as an easier method of exposition. Mr. A. was still lying on the bench, relaxed and quiet. I still had one hand on the crown of his head, the other on his solar plexus. "This process," I said, "calls for an even stronger effort on the part of your imagination. First of all, I want you to visualize your brain. You've seen diagrams and drawings of the brain often enough to know what it looks like - a mass of gray and white substance, convoluted and twisted in upon itself, divided into two hemispheres, with a front and rear portion. Picture it, and hold it firmly in your mind, then tell me what happens, if anything."

Mr. A. took a little time for this unaccustomed mental effort. Finally he said, "It seems as if that sort of muddled feeling I've had so long that I'd gotten used to it, were going away. I feel clear-headed. There's a warm feeling spreading out from the center of my skull - and a sort of tingling, pins-and-needles feeling, but not painful."

"Now," I said, "try to visualize blood flowing down the

forehead from the brain to the eyes. You've seen the kind of chandelier that has an opaque glass bowl suspended from four chains?" Mr. A. nodded.

"Imagine that your eye-balls are the glass bowl, and the muscles behind your eyes the four chains. Got the picture?" He nodded again.

"Then imagine the blood descending from the brain down those four chains, warming them and relaxing them so the eyeball sinks gently back into its socket."

"The idea of chains," said Mr. A., "makes the picture perfectly simple. It doesn't take any effort to imagine it."

"You'll find," I said, "that it becomes even simpler with practice, so that pretty soon you only have to think of relaxation, and the effect is achieved instantly."

"That's good," said Mr. A. appreciatively, "I don't mind admitting that all this imagining is a little tough, at first. My imagination isn't used to this much work, I guess."

"Then it's high time it was limbered up." I was only half joking. "You saw, in the first part of the treatment, how easily I limbered up your arms and legs and trunk with my hands. That was only a beginning, for, as you've seen since, there are a lot of tensions that can't be reached with your hands. The imagination can, and does, do the work just as well. Since your imagination doesn't take up any space, and knows no barriers, there is no nook or cranny in your body that it can't reach. So let's put it to work again.

"We've started on your head, so let's finish it up. Don't try to hurry this process - the more thorough the process of flushing various areas with blood - which, incidentally, we call dirigation - the more complete and efficient the relaxation will be."

"I'll need a little more practice before I could hurry it." Mr. A. confessed. "It's a new idea to me, and it takes a little getting used to."

"That's all right," I assured him. "It's worth spending some time on. Now - visualize the blood flowing down to the temples, the ears and the cheek bones. Follow with the visualization of the nose, mouth, lips, tongue, chin, jaws. Feel how your whole head has become suffused with blood, and how it has produced a spontaneous relaxation of every muscle, organ and nerve in the entire head. Slowly, very slowly."

"I feel as if I were blushing like a school girl," Mr. A. admitted sheepishly.

"Yes, it really does. It's amazing what your imagination can do."

"It is," I answered, "so amazing that it's a crime to let the imagination go completely to waste, as the majority of people do. Now apply yours to your throat - think the blood into the larynx and the pharynx. Imagine it flowing to the thyroid glands at the base of the neck. This process will help stimulate this gland into balanced activity, assisting normal metabolism. If the thyroid is defective, repeated flushing with blood will help eliminate the defect. If it's overactive, this relaxation will tend to normalize its function.

"Now continue the imagining until the blood pours into the chest and stimulates every single cell of the entire lung area into renewed activity, and relaxes the vessels and nerves and muscles in that region. Visualize the heart in the middle of the chest, hanging over toward the left side. You can relax it as you learned to relax the other organs."

"I keep being surprised," said Mr. A., "to find that this really works. My breathing seems fuller, and more effortless, since I imagined the blood pouring into my chest and lungs."

"Definitely, it really works. Even such things as high and low blood pressure can often be restored to normal by this method. Now that you've got the general idea, I'll be brief. Flush the muscular wall of the stomach and liver, and their surrounding glands. Visualize your kidneys, lying behind the stomach, almost against your back. Imagine the two small glandular bodies above the kidneys - the supra-renal glands. Imagine them being stimulated by the flow of blood so they pour a copious supply of energy into the bloodstream.

"Follow this by the visualization of the abdomen and lower part of the trunk containing the small intestines, colon, and part of the genito-urinary system. Make sure in your own mind that you give enough time to visualize the flow of the blood."

The more you relax the middle area of your body, the more likely it is that the whole of your body will be relaxed. Dr. Georg Groddeck, one of the most brilliant psychologists, called the abdomen together with the rich nerve supply and the instinctual impulses that seem to emanate from it, the "middle man" of the body. In the eloquent imagery and symbolism that this brilliant physician employed, this middle part of the body was conceived to be endowed with a species of mind even as the breast and the head - this "belly-mind" being often opposed to the inclinations and rational activities of the head-mind. It is the seat of sexual instincts, feelings and passions, and all the dynamic instinctual forces inherited from the past, that we consider in psychology to be resident in the "unconscious," or the "Id" as Freud calls it.

Because of the direct interaction of mind and the physiological functions of the body, if the body is assisted to relax, a direct effect is produced within the consciousness and visa versa. I will prove this point later at great length and to some effect. At this moment it is imperative only to

THE LAZY MAN'S GUIDE TO RELAXATION

emphasize the fact that by completely relaxing the middle part of the body, the abdomen and all that it implies, you go far toward relaxing the basic conflict that exists in most of us. It is an internecine warfare between the primitive instinctual part of our make-up and the surface consciousness which we consider to be ourselves. The conflict is overcome by doing no more than once was done in the words, "Peace! Be Still!"

Finally, visualize the blood separating into two powerful streams, two rivers of blood descending from the abdomen into the thighs and legs. Actual anatomical pathways are indicated in this connection. Be very attentive here too; visualize all the tight, stiff, taut thigh and leg muscles thoroughly, in order to relax them under the stimulus and warm influence of the blood. In this manner, proceed gradually until the toes are reached. Now pause.

THE SENSE OF ENJOYMENT

You have completed a great cycle in the relaxing process. Pause to consider and observe. Note how you feel. Record your feelings. Permit the sense of real pleasure and enjoyment and freedom to make an indelible impression upon your mind. If the memory of this experience is well recorded, it can be evoked at any moment from your storehouse of memories. It matters not if you ride in the subway, are seated in a car or plane, or are sitting at home reading or listening to the radio or T.V., you have only to remember the pleasure of relaxation that you obtained from these repeated experiments and forthwith the memory is evoked from your consciousness impacting itself upon the cells and tissues and fibres of the body. Relaxation then follows.

Relaxation ensues because you have thought relaxation. It is a physiological fact that to think of a certain part of the body is to cause the blood to flow there. I shall show that any thought produces some bodily change, chemical or dynamic. These phenomena, over a reasonable length of time, become associated in the subconscious depths of the mind and co-ordinate with one simple idea - relaxation. Consider this fact. Visualize the phenomenon. Then behold it, it is there.

"As a man thinketh in his heart, so is he." So wrote a master of life. We can do no better than to heed his words, following them to the end.

The fourth stage of the relaxation technique is comparable to the foregoing. We continue the active employment of the imagination or image-making faculty. Very early in our practice of relaxation, we discover the enormous importance and value of this eidetic faculty of our minds. It is easy to understand why some writers have considered this faculty the poetic and creative faculty par excellence. Some have gone so far as to suggest that the genius is one gifted with a keen visual imagination and a surplus of nervous energy. If this be the case, it is my contention that in relaxation we have a ready-make method whereby we can evolve, not necessarily genius, but men and women whose health, ability and spiritual capacity are considerably beyond the normal.

We have seen that energy is disposed to develop or to increase itself to an extraordinary degree under the stimulus of the proper relaxation devices. Moreover, we have seen that imagination has a marked effect on bodily processes, especially nervous processes, and that the imaginative faculty is capable of considerable development simply by being used. You will soon discover that by adhering to the few rules given here, you will become adept in visualizing the different organs of your body, and any other thing that you wish to visualize. Not only will this art of relaxation give you a degree of control over your bodily processes as well as an enhancement of physiological function and health generally, but you will find also that you are provided with a potent means of self-culture, the value of which is not to be underestimated for one single moment. At the beginning of this book I said, "Be yourself!" If you have been scrupulously careful and honest in these exercises, you will understand something of what is meant by this expression, "Be yourself!" When you relax you are more nearly yourself than at any other time. You will come to realize what you are and what your innate abilities are. By means of the imagination utilized during this state of quiet, you will learn how to make them explicit and how to make them manifest themselves. In this fourth stage of the process, we are confronted by an experience which has been commonly called "the influence of mind over matter." I dislike this glib phrase. It offends me enormously, even though I am disposed to accept the truth implicit in it.

One is reminded too strongly of cults and mind-healing systems whose unscientific methods of operation have had the tendency to bring disrepute to most of the legitimate therapeutic systems. At the same time, however, facts are facts, in spite of the coloring or interpretation given them. We find, if we approach the subject in an open-minded manner, that by mental activity we produce not only a deeper and more profound state of relaxation useful to increased bodily health and mental poise, but we discover also that mental processes have a remarkable influence on physiological function.

MOODS AND THE BODY

We are, most of us, familiar with such recorded experiences of getting a phone call with bad news while enjoying a meal. The result may be a violently disturbed state of the gastro-intestinal tract. Or, there is the case of the helpless maniac, wrapped in gloom and inertia, weak, and lost to the world - who, all of a sudden, when some idea enters his mind, may be possessed with the strength of ten men. It is well-known that reading provocative literature will produce a marked stimulation of the sex organs of either sex. All these things tend to indicate that feelings and ideas may be projected into the body system causing them to react there with some effect. The therapy dealing with this type of thinking is called "psychosomatic medicine."

Psychosomatic means mind-body. The implication is that moods, which are protracted emotional reactions, are capable of producing a physiological response in the form of altered functions. A shock appears to stimulate the adrenal glands to pour forth epinephrine (a glandular hormone) into the blood stream. The hormone is carried to the body organs which respond in a certain manner. The cardiac rate is accelerated to hasten the output of blood through the heart muscle. Breathing is faster, the skeletal muscles tighten, and peristalsis is arrested or retarded. This is a readiness for fight or flight - the emergency response - physical and psychic, to any situation creating fear. If, through a wide variety of causes, this attitude becomes protracted or habitual, then actual organic or architectural changes, physically speaking, may be instituted, requiring psychosomatic treatment - from both points of view.

To be successful, everyone requires a thoroughly relaxed body. It is necessary and useful to repeat at this time the technical methods given at the beginning for inducing a degree of physical and mental quiescence before performing these simple experiments.

CHAPTER SIX

THE LAZY MAN'S GUIDE

Lie down, with fingers interlaced and legs crossed at the ankles. Start to breathe very slowly, deeply, and rhythmically. Let your inhalation be felt to the deepest portion of your lungs. Inhale to a measured cycle of about four seconds, counting very slowly in your mind. Exhale slowly and completely to the same rhythm. This process is named rhythmic breathing and its effects are salutary. One sign of success is a quiet rippling over the solar plexus with a marked sense of warmth and enormous power invading one's body even in absolute repose. This sensation should certainly be present before proceeding to the next step. This sensation should be produced without undue effort.

Next imagine that you, like Alice lost in Wonderland, have eaten a fragment of some magical cake that causes you to shrink. Build up in your mind strong and vivid pictures of this act of shrinking. See yourself getting smaller and smaller. Now, visualize yourself as hardly more than a minute speck. I know this may sound nonsensical, even fantastic, and I do not even ask that you believe anything. I only ask that you experiment scientifically and observe what happens.

As you tend to shrink in your imagination, pay attention to the rate and type of your breathing. Whereas previously your breath was full and deep, in this experiment of growing smaller and smaller, you will note that your breathing becomes shallower and more superficial. This is not a dogmatic statement. Try it yourself, experiment with it. Notice the effect it has not only on your breathing, but on your control of self and your ability to relax easily and profoundly. When you have shrunk so completely that further thought of shrinking is impossible, try to conjure up in your mind a memory of yourself at the beach, for instance. It is summer, and you are lying prostrate on the beach. Your eyes are closed tight, your arms and legs flung out, you are relaxed. You suddenly experience the sensation of falling. The earth is whirling downwards in space and you are whirling and falling with it. Can you recall the distinct sense of falling downwards and backwards from the head, as it were? Conjure up this recollection, and like this memory, try to feel that you, this minute speck, this point, are falling in infinite space.

It will give you a sense of untrammelled and undreamed of freedom. Throughout this experiment be self-collected and note what effect it has upon your breathing. It will change regularly and inevitably with each chain of thoughts and images that flit before your mind. When you feel you can fall no more, you will come to rest spontaneously. Imagine you have found your own center somewhere in space. To this center converge all the forces of the universe; light rays, cosmic rays, and whatever other rays of force and light that you can conceive of. You are a small point centered somewhere in the vast emptiness of space, and focussed upon you is the whole universe. Feel, how you, the tiny speck - become invaded by cosmic energy and power and light from without. It permeates you through and through. Continue this process until you feel the impact of energy upon you with a fructifying effect causing you to grow.

Slowly, you grow larger and larger. Soon you reach your normal size. Stop for a moment to observe the effect of these visualizations upon your breathing. The rate of inspiration is rapid and very full - as though the attempt mentally to grow large had an exhilarating effect upon the emotional mechanisms of your breathing process. Observe also your own reactions as to alertness and intellectual clarity. You feel extraordinarily vital, as though an unlimited supply of energy had somehow become available. The entire body is throbbing and tingling with power. Besides this, the mind itself is still and quiet and crystal clear, as though it felt no problem could be too large or complex or difficult for you to solve.

PRACTICE MAKES PERFECT

This is no mere rhetoric. Are these results worth while? Personally, I think so, I believe you will too, after you have acquired some experience. You will come to feel as I and many others have come to feel, that in knowing this technique, the whole tenor of life has been altered and changed very much for the better. It will become infinitely easier to express what you are. The mask of self-deception that firmly encases one drops away, and the real personality, free from the dross of fantasy and gross limitation, is there for all to see.

One very intuitive psychological exponent has said that the entire object of psychoanalysis and analytical psychology was to confront the individual with himself and enable him to see and to accept himself as he actually is without any fond illusions and fantasies. By means of a prolonged analysis of one's past history and his relations with his family, and an examination of present day reactions to any and every circumstance and event that arises, he is rid of the false mask that blinds him to himself, eliminating the shell of fantasy in which he is deeply confined. This being the case, it will be seen that relaxation accomplishes somewhat similar ends to those of psychoanalysis without the strain that attends the latter, especially as concerns time, money, and emotional upset.

THE LAZY MAN'S GUIDE TO RELAXATION

This is an interlude only. We are dealing with the experiment of enlarging oneself in the imagination and watching the reaction subsequently, upon the personality. Having reverted to normal size, once more conceive yourself in the same situation as did Alice who is lost in the perplexing and bewildering events of Wonderland. Once she became too small but began growing large again when she ate some cake. Imagine yourself, too, growing larger and larger. Whereas before, your shrank to an infinitesimal size, you now are slowly expanding to almost infinite dimensions. So extensive have you become that all space is filled. Imagine that all the heavenly bodies, the entire totality of stars, suns, and planets are so many specks within your body. Include them all in the same way as the minute cells make up the organs and limbs and other tissue of your body. Again, notice what result this notion has upon your breathing. Your breathing should be extraordinarily well-rounded and full.

If at any time in your life you ever complained of inferiority or lack of poise, of emotional imbalance or irrational fears, these aspects of personality gradually vanish from your character entirely. Your emotions and mental faculties are being developed and relaxed by the practice of these exercises; as a result, a new poise and dignity grow on you. Your health, too, undergoes a general improvement. Neurasthenia? What chance has nerve exhaustion of surviving such a mode of discipline? A host of minor ills disappear in the face of this dynamic charging of the human frame.

Why do I constantly enjoin you to watch your breathing? Because you take in oxygen when you breathe. Oxygen is life and it promotes life. If you breathe with but one-half or less of your full lung capacity, how can you be well? Or dynamic? How can you be yourself? Under the stimulus of relaxation, the instinctual energy latent in the cells themselves enable the cells to respond to their innate pattern, and thus stimulate the entire lung as an organ to renewed activity. Every cell thus becomes exposed to the incoming oxygen and is stimulated to throw off the residual carbon dioxide. Thus new oxygen is passed into the bloodstream in larger quantities. This reacts upon the pulsing of the heart. The heart pumps the blood through the arterial system more vigorously only when the blood is not being adequately oxidized. With proper oxidation, the heart works without strain - it automatically relaxes. A similar effect is exerted on the muscular walls of the arteries and veins, and other blood vessels.

Since the blood carrying oxygen goes to every part of the body, no matter how remote, we can see that this relaxation mechanism produces an indirect effect upon the most distant cell and upon the farthest nerve and body tissue. That is why I insist that you watch how you inhale and exhale. Your lungs respond at once to these subtle changes that occur within your mind. The lungs affect your entire body by reflex action. Hence, what you think produces some change at once within your body.

AHHHHH!

THE LAZY MAN'S GUIDE TO RELAXATION

Let me develop this theme a little futher. The late L.E. Eeman, whom I consider to have been one of the greatest authorities on relaxation, made a discovery which emphasizes this idea in a way rather different from my development of it as indicated in the foregoing. Take a sheet of paper and on it draw the human torso from shoulders to hips. Divide this horizontally into seven transverse sections by drawing several straight lines from side to side. Between the lines in each space, write the colors of the solar spectrum: begin first with red, then orange, yellow, green, blue, indigo, violet. This is your basis for further experimental work.

COLOR AND RELAXATION

First, relax as before. Be certain you are conscious of and relaxed of every conceivable tension. Relaxation obtained, visualize the color red. Visualizing a fire engine or a field of poppies in bright sunlight, or a length of flaming red silk may help you in this process. Stare at the picture you conjure up for several seconds. Notice the almost immediate effect this has on your breathing. Your breathing is rapid, it is high, the so-called clavicular breathing. Consult your diagram of the torso. You find the color red occupying the highest transverse section. It corresponds to the area of the chest where the greatest motion takes place when red is visualized.

Drop the whole series of pictures. Wait for several seconds, heave a sigh or two, then imagine the color blue. A length of blue silk, the color of the sky on a clear summer's day, a bed of blue flowers, or anything that is blue in color, like some of the airplanes of one of the major companies. Hold the image for a while, afterwards transferring your attention to the movement of your lungs. Instead of being rapid and clavicular, it tends to be deeper and much slower. The lower the color in the spectrum chart, it seems the lower down is your breathing when you visualize the color. Visualize all the colors of the spectrum, one at a time.

You will discover that which Eeman discovered: that these colors affect your breathing according to their place on the spectrum chart you have drawn.

Why this is, I don't know. One could invent many explanations, all equally valid. This is neither the time nor the place for speculation about this. We are concerned only with the fundamental observation. By thinking a certain specific thought, a specific reaction is induced in lung action. Your entire metabolic process, consequently, is susceptible to physical and chemical changes brought about by your mental processes.

This is a most important discovery. If you imagine yourself listening to the booming of a bass drum or to distant church bells, your breathing is low. The sound of a violin or a piccolo, on the other hand, causes you immediately to breathe rapidly and very high up in the chest. Visualize shapes, and note how the image of a circle affects you as opposed to a square or a triangle or a rectangle. Note also, the effects of different tastes such as acid, sweet, sour, and salt - these produce totally different reactions. If they are willing, try this idea on your family, your friends, acquaintances. In fact, try it on all the people you know. At first, NEVER tell them the theory or what they may expect. For, when changes occur in their breathing, their usual retort is, "suggestion!" What

THE LAZY MAN'S GUIDE TO RELAXATION

this means, I confess I do not know. It is too glib and irresponsible an answer. Those who use it are ignorant of both the significance of suggestion and the method they are trying to criticize. Only when you have produced the results expected should you acquaint them with the facts. They will be just as puzzled as you about the whole matter.

The phenomenon itself is far more important than any explanation of it might be. Your object is to make use of it and employ it to your own ends. The fact that pictures of color, of sound, and of shape are able to produce an effect upon your breathing has far reaching results which become evident to anyone after a little exploration in this field of relaxation.

CHAPTER SEVEN

FOR THOSE WHO ARE REALLY LAZY

One more set of relaxation exercises remains to be described; then I will burden you no more. I regard this last set of exercises as very important and its results as most effectual. You have just now finished the first phase of the technique and are at this moment thoroughly relaxed and ready for the next step. Your ankles are crossed and your hands are resting easily upon the abdomen with fingers interlaced.

As you know, the entire body covering, the skin, is punctured all over its surface by large numbers of tiny orifices called pores. These pores serve many physiological purposes. While relaxing, think of these pores not as minute openings, but as large holes that are wide open. It will be easy to imagine this if you mentally cope with the idea in small areas. For example, think of the skin on your face, of the skin on your cheeks. Picture clearly and vividly the small pores stretching and stretching until they gape. If your visualization is good, you obtain a distinct stretching sensation of the skin. The mechanism involved seems to be that the motor nerves convey electrical impulses from the brain to the muscles and the skin of the face to which they respond. Extend the field of your operation to the forehead, the scalp, and all of the head and neck. Be certain that you feel the queer, little prickling sensations which mark the opening of the orifices of the pores, before proceeding.

I THINK I MAY HAVE CARRIED THIS "SKIN" STRETCHING RELAXATION TOO FAR!

DO NOT HURRY. It is better to complete a whole process in a small area than to rush the experiment over the entire body in a haphazard and careless manner. Continue similarly with the skin of the chest and abdomen, with the skin of the back, the thighs, and the legs. Pause every once in a while to observe the effect of this pore-stretching exercise on the general relaxation.

Turn your attention again to the brain and head. Just as you visualized the skin as being full of holes, now imagine the content of the head as being full of holes. Think of a large swiss cheese, or a sponge. This will help you in your aim. Tell your head that you feel it has suddenly become full of holes, that it now feels exactly like a sponge. Extend the same concept to the neck, the torso, the legs, and the feet. By this time your internal organs are converted into large, living masses of sponge. Now follows the fascinating development of this conversion. You are full of holes - completely full of minute orifices bound together by a network of protoplasmic tissues. The atmosphere is on the outside. Air is above, below, and around you. At this point, feel that you must eliminate whatever vacuum may exist in these spaces within you.

So you bid, imaginatively, the currents of air that surround you, to flow through your body in every direction. The spaces are now filled with air, with life-giving, energy-producing oxygen. Imagine, too, that winds are blowing through your body from various directions; from the feet through the body to the head, and vice versa. Feel a breeze entering your body from above and blowing through you. Reverse the order and interchange the directions. Use all the ingenuity of which you are capable and produce imaginary movements of air or energy through the interstices within your own frame. Take a very deep inspiration -- and imagine you are inhaling not only through your nose but also through the enlarged orifices in the soles of your feet. The air rushes through them all the way up your thighs and abdomen into your chest.

Exhale in the reverse manner. Inhale air through the crown of your head; through the small of your back.

Fantastic? Of course it is. I would be the last to deny it. I do not mean to imply that this process actually takes place. What I do definitely assert, however, is that somehow, for various obscure reasons, a distinct relaxation of body tissues takes place through these imaginative efforts, and a circulation of different biological energies is set in motion. A sense of freedom, of lightness, a clarity of insight, and an extraordinary vitality develops from these experiments in relaxation that are unlike anything you may have experienced in all your life. The directions are not difficult. It is easy to relax in this way. The results that accrue to you are inestimable.

THE LAZY MAN'S GUIDE TO RELAXATION

You relax the body, the benefits extend to the mind. You develop the ability to relax physically as well as to relax emotionally, as is noted in your relaxed attitude towards the events of life. All the tension that existed in your mind regarding people, experiences, and life generally, are overcome. Slowly, you learn how to let life itself work upon you. If only you let it, it will transform you and bless you. If only you give it half a chance, nature will alchemically transmute you, whereas before life only hardened and hurt you. You will learn not to fix your mind into a rigid, unyielding mold that will be in dire conflict with the changing, fluctuating world without.

Rather, you will learn to "sit loose to life," becoming a child of the moment. By doing this, you discover a new world of happiness opens up to you. You discover also, a thing of surpassing interest -yourself. What a discovery! You are yourself once more! You are now a traveller on the high road of noble adventure. With an indescribable serenity, peace and harmony, you discover the world anew.